part 1

beauty basics

suit yourself:
your features

Forehead

Some people think theirs is too big. Others think it's too small. You could conceal it with bangs, but we say pshaw. Small foreheads are cute and dainty as is. Big, wide ones make you look smart. Accessorize with some stylish glasses and you'll have brainy beauty.

Eyes

Play up your eyes by enhancing their natural shape. If you're lucky enough to have large eyes, frame them with a touch of dark eyeliner. If they're small, bring them out by lining them in a light color. If they're close-set, use shadow to emphasize the outer third of the eye. Beautiful wide-set eyes look nice when shadow emphasizes the inner third.

Nose

Everyone hates her own nose. It's either too long, too short, too pointy, too snub, too wide, or too bumpy. And it's too bad, after all your nose does for you. It allows you to smell flowers and fresh cookies, and it gives you something to rest your shades on. Love your nose! If you can't, you have two options: Draw attention elsewhere, with dramatic lip or eye makeup, or contour it with a mix of foundation colors. But be warned: Contouring is really useful only for photo shoots. In daylight, your nose will just look dirty. If you've got a nose with character, consider yourself lucky. Strong features make you a rare and exotic beauty. We'd much rather be a bird-of-paradise than a boring old daisy.

Lips

Lips come in all shapes, and they're all beautiful in their own way. We suggest you stick with the lip line nature gave you and enhance it with a little shine or color. But if you're really dissatisfied with your natural lip shape, remember that dark, matte colors make lips look smaller, and light, glossy colors make them appear bigger. Experiment with different shades until you find one that suits you.

continued on next page

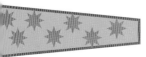

Bone Structure

Your face is perfectly sculpted just the way it is, and most attempts to change it will backfire. But you can highlight what you have with a little subtle blush. If your face is round, apply blush to the inner third of the face. If your face is long, apply blush on the outer third of your face, low, along the bottom of your cheekbone.

Freckles and Moles

We think freckles are just adorable and should be left as is. Lemon juice won't bleach them, and covering them up with thick foundation will only make you look pasty. But if you like, you can tone them down with a light, sheer foundation. Better yet, play them up with a sheer, shimmery powder. As for that beauty mark, it's just that: beautiful. But if you're really bored with it, go ahead and cover it with a dab of concealer. Then, if you like, add a faux Cindy-style mole over your lip or a Marilyn mole on your cheek. It'll be as though your mole has magically moved. Spooky beauty!

Braces

You could keep your mouth shut for the next two years, but sooner or later you may want to eat or say something. So go ahead and smile your sparkly grin with confidence. Make the most of your metal by playing it up with glitter gloss.

your coloring

You can hold up fabric swatches until you're blue in the face, but the best way to find the makeup colors that suit you is through trial and error. Expect lots of trial and lots of error. Remember that metallic purple lipstick you tried last year? The orange eyeshadow? The red mascara? No one can say you don't take risks. You can minimize your investment by using testers and shopping at stores that allow returns, and by bringing along a brutally honest friend.

Once you find colors that work for you, see how they work together. You may look good in both green eyeshadow and red lipstick, but you probably won't look good in both at the same time. A rule of thumb is to confine color to one feature only. If you're doing a colorful eye, keep the lip color neutral. If you're doing a dramatic mouth, skip the eye makeup. It's a good idea to go easy on color in general. You're young and healthy—you've got plenty of coloring to begin with, lucky thing. When in doubt, remember: You can never go wrong with clears and sheers. And when color calls, use the guide on the following pages to find the shades that will make you shine.

19

continued on next page

Pinky Fair

You have pale skin without a hint of sallowness, ash-toned hair, and blue eyes. You're fresh and fair. Dramatic colors can wash you out, so keep it pale and pretty with these colors.

Lipcolor: Pink, raspberry, rose. Burgundy lipstick is not for you, but you can probably get away with a classic red on special occasions. If you just love dark colors, try sheers.

Eyeshadow: Taupe, light gray, pink. For a party eye, try lilac.

Peachy Fair

You have warm, pale skin, light hair with gold highlights, and green or topaz eyes. You're a golden girl who sparkles in pale, warm colors. Blue notes aren't for you, but sunny tones light you up. Try these.

Lipcolor: Sheer peachy pink, caramel, light brownish red.

Eyeshadow: Gold, fawn, apricot, tea green, ivory.

Freckly

You've got coppery hair, pale skin, golden eyes, and freckles, freckles, freckles. You already have a lot of natural, gorgeous color, so you don't need to glop much more on. Let your natural beauty shine through with a little light brown mascara and a touch of lip gloss. Or try these colors.

Lipcolor: Brownish red, brownish pink, caramel.

Eyeshadow: Brown, apricot, gold, champagne. Or get crazy with green or plum.

Olive

You've got a medium complexion, dark eyes, and dark hair. You smolder with deep, rich color. Skip the pastels—they're too wimpy for you. And stay away from gray. Try these shades instead.

Lipcolor: Mauve, raisin, brick, chocolate, caramel.

Eyeshadow: Brown, gold, fawn.

Raven

You've got pale, blue-toned skin and blue-black hair. You're a dark and mysterious beauty who sparkles in any jewel tone. Stay away from yellowy tones. Stick with these instead.

Lipcolor: Don't be afraid of the dark. You look great in classic red, wine, and plum. When you want to go lighter, choose a blue-based pink. Avoid warm browns and caramels.

Eyeshadow: Silver, gray, taupe, purple.

Dark and Deep

You've got a warm, dark complexion, snapping dark eyes, and deep dark hair. Enhance your gorgeous coloring with colors that make you glow. Skip the pastels and head for the deep end. These colors will bring out your best.

Lipcolor: Blackberry, chocolate, brick red, black cherry, caramel.

Eyeshadow: Purple, plum, shimmery brown, gold.

Tawny

You've got a golden skin tone, topaz eyes, and light to dark brown hair. Complement your golden skin tone with warm, shimmery shades. Choose yellow-based colors over blue-based ones—they'll bring out your natural glow. Try these.

Lipcolor: Plum, berry, caramel, bronze, classic red.

Eyeshadow: Fawn, champagne, gold, lilac.

skin care

Before you put on the paint, you need to prime the canvas. Don't worry—it's easy. Keeping white shoes clean and linen pressed is hard, but keeping your skin clean is a snap. All you need are some supplies and a tiny bit of discipline. (That said, there are some things your crafty super powers are no match for. If you have severe acne, rashes, or other persistent skin problems, you'll need to see your friendly dermatologist.)

Healthy skin starts with healthy eating. Yes, that means veggies. No, ketchup doesn't count. And be sure to wash it all down with lots of water—it'll keep you hydrated inside and out. Stay out of the sun as best you can, and wear sunscreen when you can't. That means every day. If you simply must have a tan, fake it with bronzer or self-tanner.

Next, you'll want to determine what kind of skin you have. If you're prone to breakouts and have shiny skin with fairly large pores, you have oily skin. If your skin feels tight and you get some flaking, you have dry skin. If you don't get many breakouts and your skin feels firm, with smallish pores, you've got normal skin, you lucky, lucky girl. And if you have both dry and oily areas, you have combination skin. It's common to have an oily T-zone (forehead, nose, and chin) with dry skin around the eyes and cheeks. If that's your story, look for products formulated for combination skin, and treat each area on its own terms. Use extra moisturizer on the dry spots and extra toner on the oily ones.

The Basic Supplies

[1] Cleanser

Start with a clean slate. Wash your face with cleanser and cool or warm (not hot!) water every day.

Oily skin: Use an oil-free cleanser. If you're prone to breakouts, get an acne-control formula.

Normal skin: Choose facial soap or a mild cleanser. If this routine starts to dry your skin out, choose another brand, or just wash once a day. Use an acne-control cleanser if you're prone to breakouts.

Dry skin: You'll need a moisturizing cleanser. If your skin still feels too dry, or if your skin is extra-sensitive, you may want to wash it only once a day.

[2] Astringent

This potion tones and tightens your pores. It's optional, but you may find that you like what it does for your skin. Pour some on a cotton ball and swipe it over your face after you cleanse.

Oily skin: Astringent is a great product for you. Choose a good one that contains witch hazel or a small amount of alcohol. You might also like tea tree oil.

Normal skin: Use a mild astringent.

Dry skin: Choose an alcohol-free formula, or skip it altogether, especially if you have sensitive skin.

[3] Moisturizer

After you've painted it up and scrubbed it down, your face needs a little nourishment. Stick to simple formulas, especially if you've got sensitive skin—alpha-hydroxy acids aren't for you. Whichever one you choose, make sure it has sunscreen of SPF 15 or higher, and wear it every day. Skip the SPF at night.

23

continued on next page

Oily skin: You may find you don't need a lot of moisturizer. But you do need sun protection. An oil-free sunscreen is ideal for everyday use. At night, use a light or oil-free moisturizer, especially on dry and delicate spots, like under your eyes.

Normal skin: Choose any simple moisturizer that doesn't irritate your skin. Use it in the morning (don't forget the SPF!) and at night. If you're feeling too greasy, try a different brand, or use it just once a day. You may also want an eye cream for night.

Dry skin: Find a good, rich cream and apply it morning and night. If your skin is sensitive, pick a noncomedogenic formula (that means it won't irritate your skin). At night, you may also want to use an eye cream.

A Word on Zits . . .

You wash, you tone, you do everything right, and you still get the occasional blemish. It happens. We're here to help. The first question: to squeeze or not to squeeze? You know you really, really shouldn't, but it's hard not to when there's an ornery whitehead staring you in the eye. Resist the urge as best you can. Instead, wash that bad boy down with some cleanser and tame it with a swipe of astringent. At this point you can apply acne medication if you like. But be warned: Sometimes this just makes things worse by drying your skin out, so you end up with a pimple *and* flakes. If you do use medication, use the plain kind—the tinted stuff looks fake. Or skip the medication and apply a dab of white toothpaste (it sounds crazy, but it works). Leave it on for 20 minutes or overnight. If you can't bring yourself to use toothpaste, you can try eyedrops (like Visine)—they'll get rid of the redness. Finally, cover it up with a touch of foundation (not cover stick), set it with powder, and try to forget it was ever there.

. . . and a Word on Facial Hair

Facial hair is a fact of life. Every girl has an occasional breakout on whisker ridge. The unibrow, the hairy mole—these things happen. Don't despair. Keep stray hairs at bay with your trusty tweezers. If you're cursed with a lot of wayward wisps, or if you've got a low pain threshold, it's worth investing in a good pair. They'll banish those bad boys with minimal misery. If you're facing a furry upper lip, you have two options: bleaching or waxing. Bleaching creams are available at any drugstore and are easy to use (though you'll want to have an adult around, and be careful: Leave it on too long and you can get a nasty bleach burn). Waxing is effective but can be tricky and messy. We like to leave it to the experts and get it done in a salon.

The Fancy Stuff

Exfoliants

Exfoliants scrub off the dead skin on top to expose the fresh new skin underneath. You shouldn't use them too often, but they're a nice treat every once in a while. Shop around for cleansing grains or scrubs until you find one you like. Or make your own from $1/3$ cup finely ground oatmeal or almond flour, 4 teaspoons honey, and $2^1/_2$ tablespoons yogurt. Leave on for 15 minutes. Rinse off with warm water, gently rubbing your face in upward strokes. If you have sensitive skin, you'll want to use only the most gentle formula, or skip it altogether.

Masks

Masks are the most fun skincare product there is. They make you look crazy while they're on and glowing after they're off. Use them whenever you're feeling blah.

Oily skin: Choose a peel mask or a clay mask. Clay masks can be really drying, so be sure to moisturize afterward. You can also make your own mask mixing 1 egg white with the juice from $1/2$ a lemon. Leave on for 15 minutes, then rinse off.

Normal skin: Use a hydrating mask if you're feeling dry, or a peel mask if you're feeling oily. You can make your own peel mask by puréeing a papaya and cooking it over low heat with one packet of gelatin and a splash of water. Let it cool fully before using. Leave on for 15 minutes, then rinse off with warm water.

Dry skin: Choose a nice, rich hydrating mask. You can make your own mixing 1 egg white and 1 tablespoon of honey with 3 tablespoons of powdered milk. Leave it on for 15 minutes, then rinse off.

faking it:
a guide to foundations, powders, and blushes

We're sure you were born with flawless, rosy skin. But then your life got a little more complicated, and late nights, homework, and hormones took their toll on your perfect complexion. Fear not. You can fake it with these fabulous products. Here's a guide on what to buy and how to use it.

Foundation and Concealers

Unless your skin tone is really uneven, you'll probably want to skip the foundation. On young skin, it can be overkill. If you do need it, choose a sheer formula or, better yet, a tinted moisturizer. Test foundation formulas on your inner wrist or lower jawline before you buy to make sure you get a good color match. Apply with a makeup sponge or your fingers, being careful to blend well at the jawline. (If foundation isn't your thing, you'll still want to keep a bottle on hand to cover up zits. It conceals blemishes much better than cover stick, which is too light.) Foundation comes in about a zillion different formulas. Here's a guide to help you find the one that's right for you.

Tinted Moisturizer

This is the best bet for young skin. It's light and sheer and will even out your skin tone while letting your natural beauty shine through. It's easy to apply because you don't have to worry so much about blending. Best of all, it nourishes your skin with all those yummy moisturizing molecules. It's especially good on dry skin. It doesn't provide much coverage, so it's best for you lucky girls who don't get many blemishes. Look for a formula with SPF protection to keep your skin looking great. If your skin is oily, choose an oil-free formula. Or make your own (page 111).

Sheer Liquid Foundation

This provides just a shade more coverage than tinted moisturizer. It won't conceal blemishes, but it will even out your skin tone while letting your natural complexion shine through. It's a good choice for girls with relatively clear skin who don't need extra moisture. It can be a little tricky to work with because it dries quickly. Practice getting it on fast, applying it to one area at a time and blending as best you can.

Oil-free Foundation

This is a great choice for anyone with oily skin. It provides pretty good coverage for blemishes and shouldn't cause new ones. Look for a silicate-based formula (heavier coverage) or a water-based formula (lighter coverage). Both go on easily. But you'll want to practice applying the stuff with a light hand and blending well, as oil-free formulas can appear masklike.

continued on next page

Cream Foundation

Unless you spend a lot of time onstage, you'll probably never need this stuff. It's heavy and oily and provides coverage they'll be able to see in the very back row. But if you have substantial scarring and normal or dry skin, it might be a great formula to try, especially for dramatic dress-up occasions like the prom.

Cream-to-Powder Compact

The most convenient formula for the on-the-go girl. You can take it anywhere, and you don't need to set it with powder. It provides medium coverage. It's best for normal skin, as it can be too greasy for oily skin and the matte finish can make dry skin look drier. It's easy to apply way too much of this stuff, so practice getting it on with a light hand. Great for touch-ups after gym class.

Iridescent Foundation

This stuff has a little extra shimmery sparkle that's great for special occasions. It can be a little much for day wear, but it will make you look luminescent at night. It gives your skin a lovely dewy effect. It's best for girls who have pretty good skin to begin with, as it can make scars or blemishes more obvious.

Liquid Concealer

Foundation should take care of most of your skin's little blemishes. But if you have dark undereye shadows, scars, birthmarks, or moles you just can't live with, you'll want to pick up some concealer. It will make those pesky imperfections disappear. The trick is making the concealer disappear, too. Dot on a tiny bit and blend gently with a finger or a makeup sponge. Look for a yellow-toned formula; it will conceal more effectively. Follow with your normal foundation or powder.

Cream Concealer

Also known as cover stick, this is heavy artillery. It's useful for covering undereye shadows, scars, moles, and birthmarks. Apply sparingly to trouble spots, being sure to blend well. If accuracy is called for, apply with a tiny brush. Follow with your normal foundation or powder.

Liquid Foundation

This stuff is portable and easy to apply. It comes in a mascara-style tube with a great little wand applicator. It doesn't offer the same coverage as cream formula, but it will easily conceal small or light problem areas. Just dab it on and blend with your fingertip if necessary. Follow with your normal foundation or powder.

Powder

Think of powder as hair spray for your skin. It sets your makeup and keeps everything under control. Match your complexion as closely as possible and choose a formula that suits your skin type. Whichever kind you use, you'll want to dust it lightly all over your face, after you've applied your moisturizer and foundation (if any).

Loose Powder

The Rolls Royce of powders. It's luxurious and gives your face a polished perfection. Apply with a big, big powder brush. You can ensure more even application by tapping the excess powder off the brush before applying.

continued on next page

Pressed Powder

Portable and convenient. We especially like translucent formulas. They even out skin tone and control shine while letting your natural complexion show through.

Shine Control Powder

If your shiny nose has you feeling like Rudolph, this is the formula for you. It will keep the glare to a minimum. Keep a compact in your backpack for touch-ups.

Moisturizing Powder

If you've got dry skin, this stuff will even out your skin tone without making you look much drier. Apply with a light hand. If you still look too powdery, remove some of the excess by running a cotton ball over your face. Moisturizing powder can make your mascara smudge, so you'll want to use it sparingly around the eyes, or switch to a waterproof mascara.

Blush

You're young, you're healthy, so your complexion is probably rosy enough. But if it's not, a little blush will help you fake it. Start by choosing the right product. The guidelines below will help. Whichever kind of blush you use should go on the "apples" of your cheeks, which you can find by smiling. You might also want to apply a little bit of blush to subtly highlight other features, like your forehead and chin. Voilà! Instant rosy glow.

Powder Blush

This type is easiest of all to apply. Just sweep it on with a big brush after you dust on your normal face powder. It's good for most skin types, especially oily (just be sure to choose a formula that doesn't contain too much oil).

Cream Blush

Cream blush is rich and yummy and long-lasting. It's especially good for dry skin. When applied correctly, it looks very natural. It can be tricky to work with because it dries quickly. Use your fingers to get it on as fast as you can, and blend it in right away. Do one cheek at a time. Use sparingly to avoid a scary doll effect. Follow with a dusting of your normal face powder.

Liquid or Gel Blush

This stuff is good for oily skin. It gives you the most color but can be tricky to blend. You may need to practice a bit. Remember that a little bit goes a long way. Apply with your fingers, acting quickly and being sure to blend well. Follow with a light dusting of your normal face powder.

Bronzer

Bronzer is basically a brownish blush that gives you a sun-kissed healthy glow. Sweep it lightly over spots the sun normally tans, like your forehead, the apples of your cheeks, your nose, and your chin. Powder bronzer is great for oily skin. Apply with a big, big brush after you dust on your normal face powder. Gel bronzer also works well on oily skin. Apply with a makeup sponge or your fingers, being careful to blend well. Follow with a dusting of your normal face powder. If you have dry skin, look for a cream bronzer, and apply it as you would a gel. Whichever formula you choose, stay away from orange tones, which tend to look fake.

the eyes have it:

lashes, brows, liners, and shadows

> Eye makeup is as old as time itself. Ancient Egyptian crafty girls believed their eye makeup had magical properties. Today we just think it makes us look better, but that's sort of magical, isn't it? Here's the 411 on what to buy and how to use it.

Lashes

Maybe it's the wand, but we think mascara is magic. It can make you look bright-eyed and polished. Unfortunately, it can also make you look raccoon-eyed and psycho. Choosing the right kind can be tricky. Try a few different formulas to find what works for you. Apply from the roots up. Wear it on the top and bottom lashes or just the top. Be warned: Going too heavy on the bottom can make you look dated. And be warned again: You need to replace your mascara every few months. It can go bad and cause eye infections.

Thickening Mascara

If you like fat lashes, this is the formula for you. The downside: It can make lashes look clumpy. Minimize clumps by applying one light coat.

Lengthening Mascara

This stuff makes lashes look long and lean. We love it, but some folks find it irritating. Cheaper formulas may cause lashes to break.

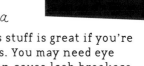

Waterproof Mascara

Smudgeproof and budgeproof, this stuff is great if you're into sports or emotional outbursts. You may need eye makeup remover to get it off. It can cause lash breakage when worn every day.

Conditioning Mascara

A great choice if you wear mascara every day. Vitamin E protects your lashes and makes them look lusher.

Clear Mascara

Cool in theory, but it doesn't do much in practice. It will set a curled lash, and it's great for keeping wayward eyebrows in place.

Eyelash Curlers

Supermodels swear by these. We think most people can live full, happy lives without them. If you're lash-obsessed, go ahead and get one—but only if you've got a steady hand. Use before you brush on mascara.

False Eyelashes

Falsies are really tricky to apply but awfully fun to wear. Here's how: Apply eyelash glue to the false lash, and give it a few seconds to set up. Position the false lash as close to your natural lash line as possible, fixing it to the outer corner of your eye first and working your way in. If the full set looks too fringy, try individual false lashes.

Brows

Begin by whipping those bad boys into shape. Shaping your brow can be tricky, so you may want to have it done at a salon the first time. If you're a real do-it-yourselfer, follow the steps below to a perfect brow. And if you're tempted to shave off all or part of your brows and draw them in instead, don't. We repeat, put down the razor and back away from the brows. You will look like an alien. Try this saner approach instead.

- Begin by brushing your brows upward and outward. Trim any long, wild hairs. Tweeze the obvious stray hairs. You'll probably find a little patch of strays just below the outer edge of your brow.

- Your brow should begin right over the inside corner of your eye and end a little bit past the outside corner. Tweeze the hairs that creep too far in either direction.

- Now locate your natural arch. It's the highest part of the brow before it starts sloping down and out toward your ear. Once you've found it, you'll shape the brow and remove the hairs that interfere with the natural arch. Think of your brows as a frame for the masterpiece that is your face, and shape them to enhance your features. A square face looks good with a rounded arch. A round face is flattered by a steeper arch. A long face looks best with a straighter line. And an oval face can get away with pretty much anything. Before tweezing, mark the hairs you want to remove with white eyeliner pencil, so you'll get an idea of how the finished brow will look.

- Get your tweezers and go for it. If tweezing makes you wince, you can numb the area by rubbing an ice cube over it for fifteen seconds beforehand. Err on the side of caution when removing stray hairs. You can always go back and tweeze more later.

Once you've got the perfect brow, keep it that way by filling in any patchy parts with brow pencil, then setting the hairs in place. You can use brow gel, clear mascara, or a dab of hair gel on a toothbrush. It sounds crazy, but nothing is better at whipping those brows into shape. Next time you're ready to retire your toothbrush, just soak it in mild detergent and hot water and say hello to your new brow brush. If you simply can't stand the thought of using a recycled tooth scrubber, buy a new brush. Just make sure it's got soft bristles.

Square

Oval

Long

Round

Eyeliners

Unless you're a rock star, you may want to skip this one. A kohl-rimmed eye is the ultimate in cool, but it can be a little much for homeroom. If you decide that liner is your look, get ready to spend a lot of time in front of a mirror. Skillful eyelining takes a lot of practice and patience. Apply liner by pulling the lid taut and drawing an even line as close to the lash as possible. Line just the top lid or the top and bottom for a real rocker chick look. Extend the top line a bit for a kitty-cat Cleopatra effect. Some people line the inner rim, but we don't love this idea—it's too easy to slip and line your cornea instead. Yuck. Speaking of yuck, be sure to replace your liquid liner every few months. It can go bad and cause eye infections.

Eyeliner Pencil

A pencil is less precise than liquid eyeliner but easier to apply. Start with a sharp pencil. Dull the tip a bit by warming it in your hand. You don't need to draw one continuous line; little continuous strokes work just as well. If the line looks too harsh, soften it with a sponge-tip eyeshadow applicator. We think pencil eyeliner looks best on the top lids only. If you want to line under your eyes as well, be sure the top and bottom lines don't meet, or your eyes will look smaller.

Liquid Eyeliner

Liquid is tough to work with but sometimes worth the effort. This stuff gives you the most precise line. It can make you look hard, but maybe that's the look you're going for. Buy a bottle (choose waterproof to prevent smudges) and practice, practice, practice.

Eyeshadow

Regular powder eyeshadow makes a great, soft eyeliner. Use a little for a natural look or a lot for a dramatic one. Dark colors like brown or charcoal look great and smoky. Crazy greens or purples can be fun, too.

White Eyeliner

Available in pencil form and easy to use. If your eyes are smallish, this will make them appear larger and more open.

Eyeshadows

Eyeshadow is where you get to have fun. It's easy to apply, and hard not to love. Who can say no to pretty colors like tea green, sparkly silver, or smoldering bronze? Use one color or a combination of several. Create a smoky eye by using a dark shadow on the outside, fading to a lighter shade as you move in. Experiment until you find a look you like.

Eyeshadow Powder

The only formula most people use or need. It's great on all skin types, and nothing is easier to apply. Use the sponge-tip applicator it comes with or an eyeshadow brush for more complicated looks.

Eyeshadow Crayon

This stuff gives you a little more control. Swipe some on your lid and smudge with your fingers to blend it in. You can also use it as an eyeliner if it doesn't go on too thick.

Eyeshadow Liquid or Cream

The colors are great, but getting this stuff on takes some practice. It can be tricky to blend. Apply with a brush or your fingertips. Liquids and creams can irritate delicate eyelid skin. If it makes your lids itchy or red, it's not for you.

right in the kisser:
lip tips

When it comes to lipwear, a girl's got choices. Creamy lipsticks, sparkly glosses, shiny sheers—sometimes we wish we had a few mouths so we could wear them all at once. Here's how to make the most of the one mouth you have.

Gloss

Gloss may be our favorite substance on the planet. It's foolproof, it smells delicious, and it gives your smile instant sparkle. No fancy techniques are required; just swipe it on. The only drawback is that it can be addictive. No one can stop with just one tube. You may want a whole wardrobe of glosses. Still can't get enough? Make your own (pages 102–105).

Clear Gloss

Your basic look for every day. Clear gloss looks great on everyone, anytime. Keep a tube in your backpack to swipe on whenever you need a little shine.

Tinted Gloss

This gives you shine with just a hint of color. It will make you look a little more grown up but not overdone. It's great for day or night.

Sparkly Gloss

Also known as party potion, this glittery stuff is great for special occasions.

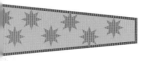

Lipstick

If lip gloss is finger painting, lipstick is high art. There are so many different kinds—which one is right for you? Experiment with different formulas until you find one you like. Or make your own (page 107–108). Whichever lipstick you choose, be sure to apply it right. Start by lining your lips. Next, fill in your mouth with your lip color, using a lip brush to apply (we know, it's much easier to simply swipe a lipstick across your mouth, but a lip brush gives you much more control). Blot. If you want the color to wear longer, apply a little powder now. Apply another coat of your color, then blot again. Smile and congratulate yourself on a job well done.

Sheer Lipstick

This transparent lip treatment gives you color without thick, pasty coverage. It's great for day. Take it with you, as it may require frequent touch-ups.

Cream Lipstick

Rich and yummy looking, this stuff gives you shine and lots of color. It's fun and goes on without much fuss. It's easy to create new colors by blending a few shades together.

Matte Lipstick

This gives you deep color without shine. Many formulas are long wearing.

Lipstick Crayon

The pencil tip allows precise application, and the colors are rich and long-lasting. The downside: It can be drying.

Lip Liner

This pencil helps define the outline of your lips and keeps glosses and creamy lipsticks in place. Choose a color that's the same as your natural lip color. A too-dark line can look harsh and unnatural.

You can also get fancy with custom color blending. Professional makeup artists smash their lipsticks into little palette tins, so they can combine colors like paint. If that sounds like too much work for you, you can achieve different colors by layering them directly on your mouth. Experiment. How do pink and beige look together? Rose and red? Plum and chocolate? Try using different shades in different places. You can get a "pout" effect by using a lighter color in the center of your lips. Try experimenting with texture, too. You can "mattify" lipstick by applying powder, or make it shiny by applying gloss. You can also get interesting effects by coloring in your whole mouth with lip liner, then applying a little gloss for shine. It's color chemistry, and you're a mad makeup scientist.

the toolbox

If your makeup kit consists of a dusty plastic bag filled with old cotton balls, dried-out mascara tubes, empty lip gloss tins, and eyeshadows you no longer wear, it's time to go shopping. You don't need to drop a lot of money in a department store. Just pick up some good, simple basics. Listed here are the supplies every crafty makeup artist needs in her toolbox.

Hardware:

Tweezers

Eyelash curler (optional)

Big powder brush

Lip brush

An old toothbrush (for brows)

Cotton swabs

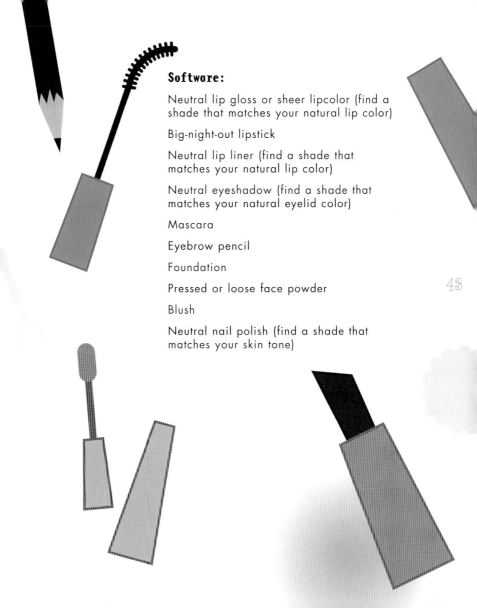

Software:

Neutral lip gloss or sheer lipcolor (find a shade that matches your natural lip color)

Big-night-out lipstick

Neutral lip liner (find a shade that matches your natural lip color)

Neutral eyeshadow (find a shade that matches your natural eyelid color)

Mascara

Eyebrow pencil

Foundation

Pressed or loose face powder

Blush

Neutral nail polish (find a shade that matches your skin tone)

part 2
natural looks

Welcome to Makeup 101. You've already learned the essential techniques; now you'll put them to use. These simple looks will help you make the most of your new makeup mastery. You'll get practice making lashes look lush and dark circles look gone. You'll become an expert lip-liner and brow-archer. You'll blush and bronze. If you're already a makeup maestro, you'll learn a few new tricks that will make you look so naturally gorgeous it'll seem as though you're not wearing makeup at all. Think of it as stealth cosmetics. No one has to know but you.

clean teen

This is your basic face, great for everyday and casual occasions. Done right, no one will know you're wearing makeup—they'll just think you're naturally this gorgeous. Some girls have all the luck.

You will need:

Blush (choose cream, gel, or powder form)

Loose or pressed powder

Brow gel and comb or hair gel and an old toothbrush

Neutral eyeshadow (optional)

Eyelash curler (optional)

Mascara

Lip liner in a shade that matches your natural lip color (optional)

Clear gloss or balm

[1] Your first assignment: Smile! This will help you find the apples of your cheeks, the firm, fleshy part that's most prominent when you're grinning. Apply a little blush to them, being sure to blend well. (If you're using powder blush, apply it after you've dusted on the powder in step 2.) Powder and cream blush are the easiest to blend. Gel blush is trickier but gives you fabulous color. Practice getting it on right, and make an honest friend promise to tell you if you look clownish.

[2] Set your makeup and smooth out your complexion with a dusting of loose or pressed powder.

[3] Comb your brows upward and outward and set them in place with brow gel. A little hair gel on an old toothbrush works just as well.

[4] If you like, you can apply a tiny bit of neutral eyeshadow. Cover the entire lid but not the brow bone area.

47

[5] Curl your eyelashes with an eyelash curler if you like. Brush on a light coat of mascara.

[6] Fill in your lips with lip liner to even out their color. Skip this step if your lips are looking pretty good to begin with.

[7] Finish with a little swipe of clear gloss or balm for just a hint of shine.

sunny bunny

So sad, but so true: There's no such thing as a healthy tan. Despair not, my pale friend. You can still acquire a golden glow. Just brush on some bronzer for a healthy, tan look.

Bronzer can be tricky. Do it wrong and you'll look like a jack-o'-lantern. Start by buying the right product. Choose a powder bronzer if you have oily skin, a cream or gel bronzer if your skin is dry. Stay away from orange tones. Once you've found a good one, apply it with a light hand. Then make up a story about an exciting weekend on a mysterious island, and you're all set.

You will need:

Loose or pressed powder

Bronzer

Big brush (if you're using powder bronzer)

Makeup sponge (optional, for gel or cream bronzer)

Shimmery neutral eyeshadow

Eyelash curler (optional)

Mascara

Copper brown lip gloss or sheer lipstick

[1] Prime your face with a dusting of loose or pressed powder. If you're using cream or gel bronzer, wait to set with powder until after step 2.

[2] It's time for Operation Instant Tan. If you're using powder bronzer, apply it with a big, big brush. Use a makeup sponge or your fingers to apply cream or gel bronzer, and be careful to blend well. You want a sun-kissed effect, so don't apply it to your whole face. Instead, just sweep lightly over spots the sun normally tans, like your forehead, the apples of your cheeks, your nose, and your chin.

[3] Apply a little shimmery neutral eyeshadow to the entire lid. Leave the brow bone area bare.

[4] Curl your eyelashes with an eyelash curler if you like. Brush on a coat of mascara.

[5] Finish with a sweep of copper brown lip gloss or sheer lipstick.

freckle face

We're sure you've been teased about them every day of your young life. Take comfort: People only tease because they're jealous. You've been blessed with hundreds of beauty marks and fantastic coloring. Go ahead and show your spots. Here's a makeup treatment that will highlight them instead of hiding them.

You will need:

Skin-brightening moisturizer (optional)

Pale pink blush

Loose or pressed powder

Eyelash curler (optional)

Mascara (choose clear or a light brown unless you have very dark hair)

Brownish pink lip gloss or sheer lipstick (if you have black or dark brown hair, a rose or berry color might be better)

[1] If you like, prep your skin by applying skin-brightening moisturizer.

[2] Apply a little blush to the apples of your cheeks, being sure to blend well. If you're using powder blush, apply it after step 3.

[3] Set your makeup and smooth out your complexion with a dusting of loose or pressed powder. This look is all about letting your natural beauty shine through, so you may want to run a cotton ball over your face to pick up the excess powder.

[4] Curl your eyelashes with an eyelash curler if you like. Brush on a coat of mascara.

[5] Finish with a little lip gloss or sheer lipstick.

healthy glow

Flowers wake up fresh and dewy. People, unfortunately, wake up dull and pasty. Happily, people have makeup. Here's a look that will highlight your features with a subtle shine. Fresh as a daisy!

You will need:

Moisturizer

Iridescent foundation or powder and a big brush

Makeup sponge (optional)

Gel blush (optional)

Eyelash curler (optional)

Mascara

Shiny lip gloss

[1] Apply moisturizer to hydrate your skin. If you're using iridescent foundation, skip this step.

[2] If you're using iridescent foundation, mix it with a little moisturizer to make it sheerer, then apply it to your face using a makeup sponge or your fingers. If you're using iridescent powder, sweep it over your face with a big brush. Concentrate on features you want to highlight, like your forehead or chin. For all-over shimmer, brush some on your neck, collarbones, and shoulders as well.

[3] Apply a little gel blush to the apples of your cheeks if you like. Be sure to blend well.

[4] Curl your eyelashes with an eyelash curler if you like. Brush on a coat of mascara.

[5] Finish with a coat of shiny lip gloss.

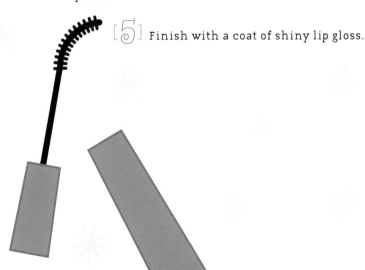

Gamine

You will need:

Concealer (optional)

Small brush, like a lip brush (optional)

Loose or pressed powder (optional)

Tweezers (optional)

Brow pencil (optional)

Brow gel and comb or hair gel and an old toothbrush

Pencil eyeliner or a dark eyeshadow

Sponge-tip eyeshadow applicator (optional)

Eyelash curler (optional)

Mascara

Lash comb (optional)

Lip balm

54

[1] If you've got dark undereye circles, cover them with concealer. Yellow-based concealers work best. Dab concealer onto the undereye area with a small brush, then gently blend, using your fingers if necessary. Set with a dusting of loose or pressed powder.

[2] If your brows need a little pruning, whip out the tweezers. Just tweeze the stray hairs; no need to pluck them to death. If they're a little patchy, fill them in with brow pencil. Comb your brows upward and outward, as neat as you please, and set them in place with brow gel. A little hair gel on an old toothbrush works just as well.

[3] Using your pencil eyeliner, line all around your eye, top and bottom. It takes a little practice, but you'll get the hang of it. Gently pull the lid taut and draw a thin, straight line. Extend the line slightly at the outer corner of the eye, to get a tame kitty effect. You can soften the line by going over it with a sponge-tip eyeshadow applicator. If that's still a little too wild for you, use a dark eyeshadow instead of eyeliner to line the eye.

55

[4] Curl your eyelashes with an eyelash curler if you like. Brush on a good coat of mascara. We don't want clumps, but we do want to know it's there. You'll get the best coverage by starting at the root and moving upward and outward. If you're still not getting the definition you want, use a lash comb.

[5] Finish with a quick swipe of lip balm, for a hint of shine.

in the pink

You will need:

Pink blush

Loose or pressed powder

Pale pink eyeshadow (optional)

Eyelash curler (optional)

Mascara

Lip liner in a shade that matches your natural lip color (optional)

Pink gloss or sheer lipstick

[1] Get your blush and paint yourself pink! Apply a rosy glow to the apples of your cheeks. Add a hint of pink color to your temples, your chin, or anywhere else. Concentrate on the features you want to draw attention to. If you're using powder blush, do this step after step 2.

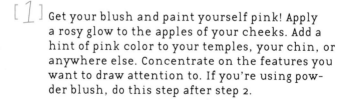

[2] Set your makeup and smooth out your complexion with a dusting of loose or pressed powder.

[3] If you like, you can apply the tiniest bit of pink eyeshadow to the eyelid, stopping short of the brow bone area. You don't want to look wall-to-wall pink, but a little shadow can't hurt.

[4] Curl your eyelashes with an eyelash curler if you like. Brush on a light coat of mascara.

[5] Give yourself a rosebud mouth with a coat of pink gloss or sheer lipstick. If you like, use the lip liner to define the shape of your mouth first. Perfect!

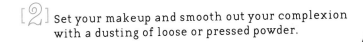

stardust

cinderella

vanity

sunburn

hot pink

classic beauty

Bored with beige but afraid of flashy fuschias? Try this look. It complements your classic features with a little clean color. It's polished and "done," but it won't make you look too made-up. It's more a genteel whisper than a shout, and it says "I look fantastic."

You will need:

Foundation (optional)

Loose or pressed powder

Brow pencil (optional)

Brow gel and comb or hair gel and an old toothbrush

Pencil eyeliner (optional)

Neutral eyeshadow (fawn and champagne are good choices; pink will clash with your lips)

Eyelash curler (optional)

Mascara

Lip liner in a shade that matches your natural lip color (optional)

Lip brush

Sheer red lipstick

fawn

champagne

[1] Cover any blemishes with a dab of foundation. Then set your makeup and smooth out your complexion with a dusting of loose or pressed powder.

[2] If your brows are a little patchy, fill them in with brow pencil. Comb your brows upward and outward and set them in place with brow gel. A little hair gel on an old toothbrush works just as well.

[3] If you like, lightly line your top lid with pencil eyeliner. Then apply a little bit of neutral eyeshadow.

[4] Curl your eyelashes with an eyelash curler if you like. Brush on a coat of mascara.

[5] If you love lip liner, go ahead and line your lips now. Then use a lip brush to apply sheer red lipstick. It's amazing what a kiss of color can do.

bright eyes

Okay, so peacock-toned eyeshadow isn't exactly natural, at least not on Planet Earth. But it's still fresh and fun and, when done correctly, totally appropriate for day wear. So go ahead and fan your feathers, lady bird.

You will need:

Concealer (optional)

Pink blush (optional)

Loose or pressed powder

Brow gel and comb or hair gel and an old toothbrush

Eyeshadow in a funky pastel: light blue or green, pink, lavender, or whatever you like

Eyelash curler (optional)

Mascara

Clear or pale pink gloss

[1] If you've got dark undereye circles, cover them with concealer.

chartreuse

bluegrass

peacock

midnight

[2] If you like, you can apply a little blush to the apples of your cheeks. If you're using powder blush, do this step after step 3.

[3] Set your makeup and smooth out your complexion with a dusting of loose or pressed powder.

[4] Comb your brows upward and outward and set them in place with brow gel. A little hair gel on an old toothbrush works just as well.

61

[5] Brush on that funky eyeshadow. Apply it to the entire lid, just up to the brow bone, blending well. Don't go nuts—a little goes a long way. Stick with one color. Rainbow combinations are for night.

[6] Curl your eyelashes with an eyelash curler if you like, and brush on a coat of mascara.

[7] Finish with a sweep of gloss.

egg plant

reckless

marilyn

moxie

part 3

nighttime glamour

Sure, daylight is nice, but we prefer night. The TV shows are better, and you get to wear much more interesting makeup. The faces in this section make the most of things. You'll practice more advanced techniques, like reshaping your brows and lips, applying false eyelashes, wearing foundation and eyeliner, using color, and creating a smoky eye. Sizzling.

bombshell baby

64

You will need:

Foundation

Makeup sponge (optional)

Pale pink or peach-pink blush

Loose or pressed powder

Brow pencil

Brow gel and comb or hair gel and an old toothbrush

Fawn eyeshadow

Shimmery white eyeshadow

Black liquid eyeliner

Eyelash curler (optional)

Black mascara

False eyelashes (optional)

Neutral lip liner

Lip brush

Cream lipstick in classic red

[1] Apply foundation to your entire face, using your fingers or a makeup sponge. Rub a little blush into the apples of your cheeks. If you're using powder blush, apply it after step 2.

[2] Set your makeup and smooth out your complexion with a dusting of loose or pressed powder.

[3] Fill in your brows with a brow pencil. Comb them into the best Marilyn-style arch you can, and set them in place with brow gel or hair gel and a toothbrush.

[4] Apply a touch of fawn eyeshadow to the eyelid. Sweep white shadow over the brow bone, blending where it meets the fawn. Use a little more white eyeshadow to line under the eye.

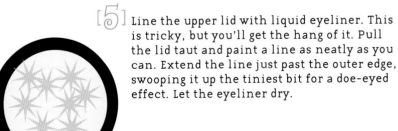

[5] Line the upper lid with liquid eyeliner. This is tricky, but you'll get the hang of it. Pull the lid taut and paint a line as neatly as you can. Extend the line just past the outer edge, swooping it up the tiniest bit for a doe-eyed effect. Let the eyeliner dry.

continued on next page

[6] Curl your eyelashes with an eyelash curler if you like. Finish with a good coat of mascara on the top and bottom lashes. If you want to go all out, you may want to wear false eyelashes instead. Simply apply eyelash glue to the false lash, and give it a few seconds to set up. Then position the false lash as close to your natural lash line as possible, fixing it to the outer corner of your eye first and working your way in.

[7] Line your lips with neutral lip liner. Use a lip brush to apply a coat of red lipstick. Blot and reapply.

66

[8] Finish by using liquid eyeliner to make a Marilyn-style beauty mark in the middle of your left cheek.

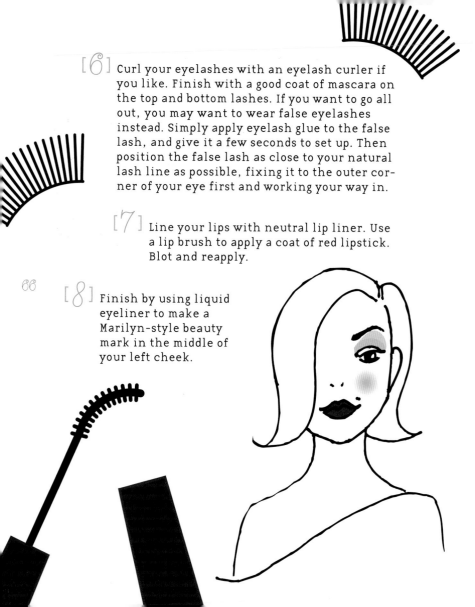

screen queen

Even if you don't have Bette Davis eyes, you can still be a black-and-white beauty. Drum up some drama with a rich lip, a smoldering eye, and a commanding brow. You oughta be in pictures.

You will need:

Foundation

Makeup sponge (optional)

Loose or pressed powder

Brow pencil

Brow gel and comb or hair gel and an old toothbrush

Chocolate eyeshadow

Fawn eyeshadow

Eyelash curler (optional)

Mascara

Neutral lip liner

Lip brush

Matte lipstick in burgundy, berry, or brick

continued on next page

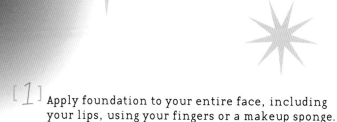

[1] Apply foundation to your entire face, including your lips, using your fingers or a makeup sponge.

[2] Set your makeup and smooth out your complexion with a dusting of loose or pressed powder.

[3] Fill in your brows with a brow pencil. It's okay to go a little overboard here. Think Joan Crawford. Comb your brows into the best movie star arch you can, and set them in place with brow gel or hair gel and a toothbrush.

[4] Apply chocolate eyeshadow to your eyelid up to the crease. Sweep fawn shadow over the brow bone and blend well. Use a little more fawn eyeshadow to line under the eye.

[5] Curl your eyelashes with an eyelash curler if you like. Brush a coat of mascara on the top and bottom lashes.

[6] Line your lips with neutral lip liner. You may want to go outside your natural lip line. Draw a full, squarish upper lip for a Joan Crawford effect. Or draw inside the lip line for a Clara Bow look.

[7] Use a lip brush to apply a coat of lipstick. Blot and reapply, then blot again.

gold dust
Woman

You've got topaz eyes and a ruby mouth. Why not set off your precious features with some gold makeup? It's twenty-four-karat beauty. Priceless.

You will need:

Moisturizer

Warm iridescent foundation or powder and a big brush

Makeup sponge (optional)

Shimmery gold eyeshadow

Eyelash curler (optional)

Mascara

Lip brush

Sheer gold lipstick

 [1] Apply moisturizer to prep your skin. If you're using iridescent foundation, skip this step.

[2] If you're using iridescent foundation, mix it with a little moisturizer to make it sheerer, then apply to your face using a makeup sponge or your fingers. If you're using iridescent powder, sweep it over your face with a big brush. Concentrate on features you want to draw attention to, like your cheekbones, forehead, and chin. For all-over shimmer, dust some on your neck, collarbones, and shoulders, too.

[3] Apply gold eyeshadow to your eyelids up to the brow bone.

[4] Curl your eyelashes with an eyelash curler if you like. Brush on a coat of mascara.

[5] Using a lip brush, apply a coat of gold lipstick. Blot and reapply.

smoldering
embers

> Set the night on fire with this smoky eye treatment. It's guaranteed to make you the toast of the campfire. Burn, baby, burn.

You will need:

Concealer (optional)

Loose or pressed powder (optional)

Brow pencil (optional)

Brow gel and comb or hair gel and an old toothbrush

Pencil eyeliner or a dark eyeshadow

Dark brown or gray eyeshadow

Light brown or gray eyeshadow

Eyelash curler (optional)

Mascara

Lash comb (optional)

Lip brush

Neutral lipstick

[1] If you've got dark undereye circles, cover them with concealer. Set with a dusting of loose or pressed powder.

[2] If your brows are a little patchy, fill them in with brow pencil. Comb your brows upward and outward, and set them in place with brow gel or hair gel and a toothbrush.

[3] Using your pencil eyeliner, line all around your eyes, top and bottom.

[4] Now you'll create your smoky eye. Apply dark eyeshadow to your eyelid, concentrating on the outer edge and fading as you move in. Use more dark eyeshadow to line under the eye. You don't want a raccoon effect, just a soft shadow. Then apply light eyeshadow to your brow bone and the inner part of the lid, being careful to blend.

[5] Curl your eyelashes with an eyelash curler if you like. Brush on a coat of mascara. Use the lash comb, if you wish, to get rid of any clumps.

[6] Using your lip brush, apply a coat of neutral lipstick. Blot and reapply.

raven

smoke

midnight

holly golightly

Who has time for complicated beauty, dahling? You're all about carefree chic. This fast face will take you from breakfast at Tiffany's to dinner at Twenty-One.

You will need:

Skin-brightening moisturizer (optional)

Peachy pink blush

Loose or pressed powder

Brow pencil

Brow gel and comb or hair gel and an old toothbrush

Black liquid eyeliner

Eyelash curler (optional)

Black mascara

Neutral lip liner

Lip brush

Peachy pink cream lipstick

[1] If you like, prep your skin by applying skin-brightening moisturizer.

[2] Apply a little blush to the apples of your cheeks, being sure to blend well. If you're using powder blush, apply it after step 3.

[3] Set your makeup and smooth out your complexion with a dusting of loose or pressed powder.

[4] Fill your brows in with brow pencil. You may want to exaggerate them a tiny bit, to get the classic Hepburn full-brow effect. Comb your brows into Audrey arches and set them in place with brow gel or hair gel and a toothbrush.

[5] Line your upper lid with liquid eyeliner. This is easier if you gently pull the lid taut. Extend the line just past the outer edge, swooping it up the tiniest bit for a doe-eyed effect. Let the eyeliner dry.

[6] Curl your eyelashes with an eyelash curler if you like. Finish with a good coat of mascara on the top lashes.

[7] Line your lips with neutral lip liner. Using a lip brush, fill in with lipstick. Blot and reapply.

heavy metal

There's nothing wrong with gilding the lily every once in a while. This over-the-top look sizzles with shimmery metallics. Heavy, baby.

You will need:

Moisturizer

Warm iridescent foundation or powder and a big brush

Makeup sponge (optional)

Metallic eyeshadow (try bronze, steel blue, platinum gray, or metallic lilac)

Eyelash curler (optional)

Mascara

Lip brush

Metallic lipstick or gloss in a shade that complements your eyeshadow

[1] Apply moisturizer to prep your skin. If you're using iridescent foundation, skip this step.

76

 steel

 chrome

 ice

[2] If you're using iridescent foundation, mix it with a little moisturizer to make it sheerer, then apply it to your face using a makeup sponge or your fingers. If you're using iridescent powder, sweep it over your face with a big brush. Concentrate on features you want to draw attention to, like your cheekbones, forehead, and chin.

[3] Apply metallic eyeshadow to your eyelid up to the brow bone. It's okay to go a little heavy; we want to know it's there. You can also use it to line under your eye.

[4] Curl your eyelashes with an eyelash curler if you like. Brush on a coat of mascara.

[5] Using a lip brush, apply a coat of metallic lipstick. Blot and reapply. Or simply swipe on a coat of gloss.

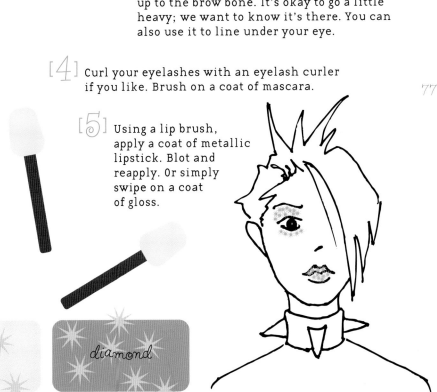

rer

diamond

wild thing

You will need:

Moisturizer

Concealer (optional)

Iridescent foundation or powder and a big brush

Makeup sponge (optional)

Waterproof pencil eyeliner

Sponge-tip eyeshadow applicator

Eyelash curler (optional)

Waterproof mascara (regular mascara will smudge)

Lash comb (optional)

Petroleum jelly

Extra-shiny clear lip gloss

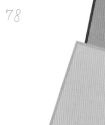

[1] Apply moisturizer to prep your skin. If you're using iridescent foundation, skip this step.

[2] If you've got dark undereye circles, cover them with concealer.

[3] If you're using iridescent foundation, mix it with a little moisturizer to make it sheerer, then apply it to your face using a makeup sponge or your fingers. If you're using iridescent powder, sweep it over your face with a big brush.

[4] Using your pencil eyeliner, line all around your eyes, top and bottom. You don't want a raccoon effect, but you do want a little drama. Soften the line by going over it with a sponge-tip eyeshadow applicator.

[5] Curl your eyelashes with an eyelash curler if you like. Brush on a good coat of mascara. You'll get the best coverage by starting at the root and moving upward and outward. If you're still not getting the definition you want, use a lash comb.

[6] Apply petroleum jelly to your eyelids, being careful not to smudge the liner or mascara. Shiny eyelids require a lot of retouching, so if you're going out you'll want to take a little more petroleum jelly with you. But it looks so cool that it's worth it.

[7] Finish with a thick coat of super-shiny lip gloss.

rock star

You're a downtown diva, a punk princess. This makeup treatment will make sure you look the part. Stare down the critics with tough-girl kohl-rimmed eyes. Curl the shimmery mouth into a beautiful sneer. Rock on.

You will need:

Moisturizer

Iridescent foundation or powder and a big brush

Makeup sponge (optional)

Pencil eyeliner

Sponge-tip eyeshadow applicator

Dark gray eyeshadow

Shimmery light gray eyeshadow (it should be almost white, but not quite)

Eyelash curler (optional)

Mascara

Lash comb (optional)

Lip brush

Sheer, frosty light pink lipstick

[1] Apply moisturizer to prep your skin. If you're using iridescent foundation, skip this step. No need for concealer. If you've got dark undereye circles, you'll look even more convincing.

[2] If you're using iridescent foundation, mix it with a little moisturizer to make it sheerer, then apply it to your face using a makeup sponge or your fingers. If you're using iridescent powder, sweep it over your face with a big brush.

[3] Using your pencil eyeliner, line all around your eyes, top and bottom. You can go a little heavy—you want them to be able to see it in the back row. Think Joan Jett. You don't want to look too neat, so smudge the line the tiniest bit by going over it with a sponge-tip eyeshadow applicator.

[4] Apply a little dark gray eyeshadow just above the eyeliner. Apply light gray eyeshadow up to the brow bone. Sweep more light gray eyeshadow under the eye for extra shimmer.

[5] Curl your eyelashes with an eyelash curler if you like. Brush on a good coat of mascara. We don't want clumps, but we do want to know it's there. You'll get the best coverage by starting at the root and moving upward and outward. If you're still not getting the definition you want, use a lash comb.

[6] Using your lip brush, apply a coat of light pink lipstick. Blot and reapply.

part 4

masquerade

Who's that girl? We're not sure, but she's obviously
a makeup genius. The looks in this section will teach
you to transform yourself entirely. You'll practice
advanced techniques: working with theatrical
makeup, applying jewels, designing a whole
new face. Think of it as a makeup master
class, and award yourself a Ph.D.
in crafty cosmetics.

goth queen

Do sunny days make you nauseous? Does pink make you itch? Does blood-red velvet make your heart sing? You've found your page. Here are instructions for your basic creature-of-the-night look. Once you've mastered it, experiment with variations. Try adding green or purple blush, colored lipstick, or eyeliner curlicues. In goth, anything goes. Well, anything except pink glitter gloss.

This is a fun makeup treatment for anyone to try. Who doesn't look good in black lipstick, heavy eyeliner, and deathly pale powder? You may never go back to glitter gloss again.

You will need:

Foundation in a color four shades lighter than your natural skin tone

Makeup sponge (optional)

Loose or pressed powder

Brow pencil

Brow gel and comb or hair gel and an old toothbrush

Black pencil eyeliner

Sponge-tip eyeshadow applicator

Eyelash curler (optional)

You will need (cont.):

Black mascara

Lash comb (optional)

Dark lip liner

Lip brush

Black lipstick

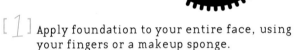

[1] Apply foundation to your entire face, using
your fingers or a makeup sponge.

[2] Set your makeup and smooth out your complexion
with a dusting of loose or pressed powder.

85

[3] Fill in your brows with a brow pencil. Comb
them into a dramatic gothic arch, and set
them in place with brow gel or hair gel and
a toothbrush.

continued on next page

[4] Using your pencil eyeliner, line all around your eyes, top and bottom. Go as heavy or as light as you like. Soften the line by going over it with a sponge-tip eyeshadow applicator.

[5] Curl your eyelashes with an eyelash curler if you like. Brush on a good coat of mascara, starting at the root and moving upward and outward. If it looks clumpy, use a lash comb.

[6] Line your lips with dark lip liner. Use a lip brush to apply a coat of black lipstick. Blot and reapply, then blot again.

glitter girl

Neutral, schmeutral. Sometimes a girl's got to sparkle. This look takes it too far, then keeps on going. And why not? No one will be able to take their eyes off you. And if the power should go out, you'll be bright enough to see by.

You will need:

Tiny flatback rhinestones (available at craft stores)

Eyelash glue

Glitter eyeshadow

Eyelash curler (optional)

Mascara

Glitter lip gloss

[1] Start with clean, dry skin. Affix tiny rhinestones to your face with eyelash glue. You'll want to keep them out of your eyes, but other than that, anything goes. Glue them in flower or curlicue shapes. Give yourself a rhinestone beauty mark. Make a dotted line above your brows. Go nuts.

continued on next page

[2] Brush some glitter eyeshadow over the entire lid and up into the brow bone area.

[3] Curl your eyelashes with an eyelash curler if you like, and brush on a coat of mascara.

[4] Finish with a sweep of glitter gloss and go sparkle.

mod squad

Style-wise, the sixties are our favorite decade. Beehives, miniskirts, macramé . . . what's not to love? We're especially crazy about sixties makeup. It's so bad, it's beautiful. The white-out mouth, the big candy-colored eyes framed by spider-leg lashes—we can't get enough. Here's how to get some swinging sixties style yourself. Groovy, baby!

You will need:

Liquid or cream foundation

Makeup sponge (optional)

Apricot blush (optional)

Loose or pressed powder

Brow pencil

Brow gel and comb or hair gel and an old toothbrush

Sky blue eyeshadow

Eyelash curler (optional)

Black thickening mascara

Lash comb (optional)

Neutral lip liner

Lip brush

Light pinky coral or white cream lipstick

continued on next page

[1] Apply foundation to your entire face, using
your fingers or a makeup sponge.

[2] If you like, apply a little blush to the apples
of your cheeks. If you're using powder blush,
apply after it step 3.

[3] Set your makeup and smooth out your complexion
with a dusting of loose or pressed powder.

[4] Lightly fill in your brows with a brow pencil. The
sixties brow is thin, pale, and rounded. Set them in
place with brow gel or hair gel and a toothbrush.

[5] Apply gobs of blue eyeshadow to your eyelids,
going up to the brow bone. If you like, use a little
more blue eyeshadow to line under the eye.

[6] Curl your eyelashes with an eyelash curler if you like. Then brush a heavy coat of mascara onto your top and bottom lashes. Prominent lower lashes will give you a really sixties look. If the mascara goes on too clumpy, use a lash comb.

[7] Line your lips with neutral lip liner. Use a lip brush to apply a coat of lipstick. Blot and reapply, then blot again.

flower child

Dig the hippie scene? This makeup treatment is a total groovy trip. The Summer of Love lives on in this funky, sunny look. There are no rules, baby, just go with what you're feeling.

You will need:

Face paint in a few different colors

Small paintbrush

Bright eyeshadow (optional)

Lip gloss

[1] Get your paint and brush and go for it. Paint a flower on your cheek, a peace sign on your forehead, a heart, a bluebird—whatever gets you going.

[2] If you're feeling the bright eyeshadow thing, go ahead and brush some of that on, too.

[3] Finish with a swipe of lip gloss for a friendly smile.

92

Miss 2103

We're crafty, not psychic. So we don't really know what the face of 2103 will look like. Maybe we'll be tattooing our foreheads and Beadazzling our chins. Maybe we'll stick to safe peachy pinks. Or maybe the face you design today will be such a hit that crafty girls will wear it 100 years from now.

You will need:

Eyeliners in bright shades, like blue, green, purple, or yellow

Eyeshadow in assorted bright colors

Mascara in colors like blue, green, or purple

Lip brush

Lipstick in assorted bright colors

93

[1] Get your eyeliners and go nuts. You don't have to limit yourself to your eyes. You can draw zigzags around your eyebrows, diamonds down your cheeks, or whatever you like.

continued on next page

[2] Brush on as many different shades of eyeshadow as you like. Do one eye green and the other one yellow. Do them both fuschia and turquoise. Brush on stripes or squiggles. Knock yourself out. Try using eyeshadow on other parts of your face. Green eyeshadow makes a lovely futuristic blush.

[3] Apply a coat of crazy mascara.

[4] Using your lip brush, apply lipstick however you like. Do the top lip pink and the bottom lip purple. Checkerboard or stripe them. Do the whole lip white with a square of blue. Anything goes!

94

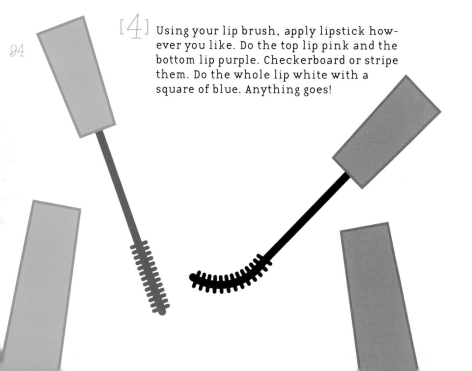

geisha girl

It takes years to learn the arts of a geisha. But you can get the look in half an hour or so. Here's how to create the classic geisha face. Accessorize with a kimono and impeccable manners.

You will need:

Moisturizer

Makeup sponge

White theatrical makeup
(available in costume shops)

Red blush

White loose powder

Big powder brush

Black eyebrow pencil

Black liquid eyeliner

Red lip liner

Lip brush

Red cream lipstick

[1] Apply moisturizer to prep your skin.

continued on next page

[2] Using a makeup sponge, apply white theatrical makeup to the entire face. Apply a touch of red blush to the apples of your cheeks. If you're using powder blush, apply it after step 3.

[3] Set the makeup with loose powder, applied with a big brush.

[4] Use your black eyebrow pencil to create a thin, arched brow.

[5] Line the entire eye in liquid eyeliner. Extend the line up at the outer corner and down at the inner corner for an exaggerated effect.

[6] Line inside your natural lip shape with your lip liner. Using a lip brush, fill in with red lipstick. Blot and reapply.

cleopatra

Historians say the real Cleopatra may have had a hooked nose, crooked teeth, a portly figure, and mannish features. All the same, she knew how to work it. A commanding eye, a mysterious mouth . . . who could resist? Work it her way with the dramatic look.

You will need:

Liquid or cream foundation

Makeup sponge (optional)

Loose or pressed powder

Bronzer

Brow pencil

Brow gel and comb or hair gel and an old toothbrush

Black liquid eyeliner

Gold eyeshadow

Eyelash curler (optional)

Black mascara

Lash comb (optional)

Dark lip liner

Lip brush

Sheer gold, goldish brown, or goldish red lipstick

continued on next page

[1] Apply foundation to your entire face, using your fingers or a makeup sponge.

[2] Set your makeup and smooth out your complexion with a dusting of loose or pressed powder. If you're using cream or gel bronzer, set with powder after step 3.

[3] Lightly sweep bronzer over your face, focusing on the cheekbones, forehead, and nose.

98

[4] Fill in your brows with a brow pencil. Comb them into an imperial arch, and set them in place with brow gel or hair gel and a toothbrush.

[5] Using your liquid eyeliner, line all around your eyes, top and bottom. Extend the line well past the outer corner of the eye for the classic Cleopatra effect.

[6] Apply gold eyeshadow to your eyelids up to the brow bone.

[7] Curl your eyelashes with an eyelash curler if you like. Brush on a good coat of mascara, starting at the root and moving upward and outward. If it looks clumpy, use a lash comb.

[8] Line your lips with dark lip liner. Using your lip brush, apply a coat of lipstick. Blot and reapply.

part 5

make your
own makeup

creamsicle
lipslicks

These tasty glosses are so creamy and frosty it's a shame they're not edible. They're not quite as refreshing as a bowl of ice cream, but they're much more portable. We all scream for lipslicks.

You will need:

2 teaspoons cosmetic-grade beeswax, finely grated (available at health food and craft stores)

2 tablespoons oil (sweet almond oil is best, but any kind will do)

1 teaspoon honey

½ teaspoon vanilla extract

1 teaspoon finely crushed powder eyeshadow in a creamy, frosty color, like pearl or pink shimmer

1 to 2 clean, dry containers (use recycled lip gloss containers or film canisters)

[1] In a small saucepan, combine the beeswax and oil over low heat, stirring until melted. Remove from the heat. Add the honey and vanilla.

[2] After the mixture has cooled a bit, stir in the eyeshadow and mix well. Cool a bit more, then transfer to the containers and allow to set.

Makes about 1½ ounces

lip fudge

You love putting chocolate in your mouth. Now you can put it on your mouth. This irresistible lip gloss smells just like chocolate fudge, and it will make you look yummy, too. It gives new meaning to a "chocolate kiss."

You will need:

1 ounce cocoa butter (available in drugstores)

1 ½ tablespoons solid vegetable shortening

2 teaspoons cosmetic-grade beeswax, finely grated (available at health food and craft stores)

½ teaspoon vitamin E oil (optional)

10 chocolate chips

2 to 3 clean, dry containers (use recycled lip gloss containers or film canisters)

[1] Combine the cocoa butter, shortening, beeswax, vitamin E oil, and chocolate chips in a small glass bowl. Microwave for about 60 seconds, until melted.

[2] Give the mixture a quick stir to blend. Transfer to the small containers. Allow to cool. If you get impatient, you can stick it in the fridge. Once it's set, you can use it. You'll be tempted to eat it, but don't: It only smells edible and is sure to make you sick. Nibble on extra chocolate chips instead.

Makes about 2 ounces

candy gloss

You will need:

2 teaspoons cosmetic-grade beeswax, finely grated
(available at health food and craft stores)

2 tablespoons oil (sweet almond oil is best,
but any kind will do)

1 teaspoon tint (use red or orange lipstick for
cherry or orange, or finely crushed yellow or
green powder eyeshadow for lemon or lime)

1 teaspoon honey

A few drops essential oil (use cherry, orange,
lemon, or lime)

1 to 2 clean, dry containers (use recycled lip
gloss containers or film canisters)

[1] In a small saucepan, combine the beeswax, oil,
and lipstick (if using) over low heat, stirring until
melted. Remove from the heat. Mix in the honey.

[2] After the mixture has cooled a bit, stir in the essential
oil and eyeshadow (if using) and mix well. Cool a bit
more, then transfer to the containers and allow to set.

Makes about 1½ ounces

space gloss

Looking for a cosmic cosmetic? This is the stuff. It's a dark and sparkly extraterrestrial substance that's pretty in an interplanetary way. Ground control to crafty girl: You look fabulous.

You will need:

1 tablespoon petroleum jelly

½ to 1 teaspoon finely crushed powder eyeshadow (choose a space-age color like blue, green, or charcoal)

Fine cosmetic-grade glitter (available in craft stores and soap-making supply stores)

1 clean, dry container (use a recycled lip gloss container or a film canister)

[1] In a small bowl, combine the petroleum jelly, eyeshadow, and glitter. Keep adding eyeshadow and glitter until you're satisfied with the color and sparkle intensity.

[2] Transfer the mixture to the container.

Makes about ½ ounce

berry lipstain

When you can't bite into a nice ripe strawberry, this concoction makes your lips look berry-stained. It smells wonderful and gives your lips a juicy, bitten look. Best of all, it's easy as berry pie.

berrylicious

106

You will need:

1 teaspoon aloe vera gel

1½ tablespoons sweetened powdered mixed-berry drink mix

½ teaspoon unsweetened powdered grape drink mix

2 tablespoons solid shortening

1 to 2 clean, dry containers (use recycled lip gloss containers or film canisters)

[1] Stir together the aloe vera gel and both drink mixes in a glass measuring cup until well mixed. Set aside.

[2] Microwave shortening in a small glass bowl on high for about 60 seconds, until melted.

sassy strawberry

[3] Pour melted shortening into powdered drink–aloe vera gel mixture. Stir until well mixed. If it separates, stir again. Once it thickens, transfer to the containers.

Makes about 1½ ounces

lipstick lab

Makeup ain't rocket science, but it is chemistry. And even if it won't get you the Nobel Prize, it can give you the lipstick of your dreams. Put your science skills to the test creating custom lipsticks you'll love. Transform your favorite matte into a gloss. Turn that heavy red into a sheer. Combine those two colors that aren't quite right to make one that's just perfect. Brilliant!

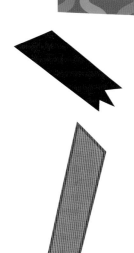

To make a sheer lipstick, you will need:

1 tube lipstick

¼-inch slice beeswax lip balm (available in health food stores)

To make a long-wearing lipstick, you will need:

1 tube lipstick

⅛-inch slice beeswax lip balm (available in health food stores)

To make a shiny lipstick, you will need:

1 tube lipstick

⅓ tube lip gloss

continued on next page

To make a new color blend, you will need:

Chunks of lipstick in assorted colors

⅛-inch chunk ChapStick (optional; it can help bind your new creation together, but you may not want or need it. Use more or less as desired)

To turn a lip liner into a lipstick, you will need:

1 lip liner

1 tube ChapStick (for matte lipstick) or 1 tube lip gloss (for shiny lipstick)

If you want to scent your lipstick, add a few drops of essential oil, like peppermint, lemon, or orange.

[1] Place your ingredients in a small glass container (the smaller the better). Microwave on high for 15 seconds at a time, until melted or melty enough to stir. Keep a very close eye on your mixture; it can start smoking. If you microwave it for a while and it doesn't melt at all, try using a different container.

[2] Quickly stir the mixture to blend, and transfer it to a mold. Use an old lip gloss container or an empty lipstick tube. Allow to set. If you get impatient, you can put it in the refrigerator.

Makes 1 lipstick

really rosy
gel blush

Nothing looks more natural and pretty than gel blush. But it can be hard to find and expensive. Why not make your own? It's a great way to use up powder blush that's too dark. You'll end up with a pretty potion that will put instant pink in your cheeks. And when your friends compliment you on your glowing complexion, it's okay to blush a bit more.

You will need:

1 tablespoon aloe vera gel, plus more as needed (available in drugstores; choose a colorless formula)

1 teaspoon finely crushed powder blush, plus more as needed

1 clean, dry container (use a recycled lip gloss container or a film canister)

[1] In a small bowl, combine the aloe vera gel and powder blush. Test some on your face. If you're not satisfied with the color saturation, add more blush or aloe vera gel as needed.

[2] Transfer the mixture to the container. Apply to cheeks, chin, or anywhere you need a little color.

Makes about ½ ounce

glitter potion

110

You don't need witchcraft to make your skin glow. Leave the cauldron alone and whip up this mixture instead. It'll give you instant all-over sparkle. Magic!

You will need:

3 tablespoons aloe vera gel (available in drugstores; it comes in green, blue, and clear)

Fine cosmetic-grade glitter (available in craft stores and soap-making supply stores)

1 clean, dry container (such as a film canister)

[1] In a bowl, combine the aloe vera gel and glitter, stir. Add more glitter until you're satisfied with the sparkle level.

[2] Transfer the mixture to the container. Apply whenever and wherever you need a little extra sparkle. You can even use it in your hair!

Makes about 1½ ounces

skin magic

If we had magical powers, we'd spend a lot of time zapping zits away. Since we don't, we have to rely on tinted moisturizer. This clever concoction isn't exactly sorcery, but it will smooth out imperfections. Abracadabra!

You will need:

2 tablespoons face lotion, plus more as needed (use an oil-free formula if your skin is oily)

1 tablespoon foundation, plus more as needed (make sure it's a good match for your skin tone)

1 clean, dry container (such as a film canister)

[1] Combine the lotion and foundation in a small bowl and mix well. Test on your face. If you're not satisfied with the coverage, add a little more lotion or foundation as needed.

[2] Transfer the mixture to the container. To wear, simply smooth it all over your face with your fingers or a makeup sponge, being sure to blend well.

Makes about 1½ ounces

tan in a
bottle

We love sunless self-tanners, but sometimes two hours is too long to wait for a tan. When we're in a rush, we cheat with this magical mixture. It's especially good on arms and legs. It gives you an instant golden glow. But be warned: It can give anything it touches a golden glow, too, so you'll want to stay off the white couch while you're wearing it.

You will need:

½ cup body lotion or aloe vera gel or baby oil gel (available in drugstores; choose a colorless formula)

2 tablespoons powdered bronzer, plus more as needed

1 clean, dry container

[1] In a small bowl, combine the lotion or aloe vera gel or baby oil gel and bronzer. Test on your skin. If you're not satisfied with the color saturation, add more bronzer or lotion as needed.

[2] Transfer the mixture to the container. Apply wherever you need warm color, being careful to blend well.

Makes about 4 ounces

novelty nails

Nail polish comes in thousands of colors, but sometimes the color you're looking for isn't one of them. When that's the case, crafty girls craft their own custom color. Make sheer pink glitter, sparkly sunshine yellow, or anything that strikes your fancy. Your ten fingers will be one of a kind.

You will need:

1 paper envelope

1 bottle white or clear nail polish

½ to 1 teaspoon finely crushed powder eyeshadow, plus more as needed

⅓ teaspoon fine glitter, plus more as needed (optional; available in craft stores)

[1] Make a tiny funnel by snipping off a corner of the envelope. Open the bottle of nail polish and position the funnel over the top.

[2] Pour the eyeshadow and glitter into the nail polish, using the funnel. Mix well. You can either stir it with the applicator brush or, if that doesn't work, cap the bottle and shake well.

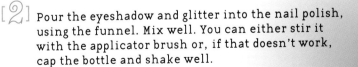

[3] Brush a little on a nail. If you're not satisfied with the color or sparkle, add more eyeshadow or glitter as needed.

Makes 1 bottle of polish

creepy cosmetics

Makeup has many uses, and sometimes pretty isn't the point. If you're going for a look that will make people go "eeuww" rather than "ahhhh," these special-effects creations are for you. Make scabs, warts, wounds, or what-have-you. Great for costume parties or really boring school days.

Scabs

You will need:

1 envelope unflavored gelatin

¼ cup cold water

Red and blue food coloring

Corn syrup

1 teaspoon cornmeal (approximately; use more or less as needed)

1 small paintbrush

[1] Combine the gelatin and water in a small saucepan and let stand for 1 minute. Heat over a low flame until the gelatin is dissolved, stirring constantly. Add red food coloring (and just a little blue) until you're satisfied with the color. Set aside and allow to cool.

[2] Dab corn syrup on your face where you want the scabs to go. Top the syrup with a thick coating of cornmeal. Let this mixture set up for a couple minutes, then carefully tap off the excess cornmeal.

[3] Test the gelatin mixture to make sure it's not hot (or else you could end up with a real scab—yuck!). Using the paintbrush, carefully and gently brush gelatin over your cornmeal formations. Allow to set. That's it. Try not to scare the kids.

Makes about 2 ounces

Hairy Warts

You will need:

Tiny hairs (use individual false eyelashes, or pull a couple of hairs out of a paintbrush)

1 whole peppercorn (use white for white warts or black for black warts)

Eyelash glue or corn syrup

[1] Glue the hairs to the peppercorn using eyelash glue or corn syrup. Allow to set.

[2] Using the eyelash glue or corn syrup, glue the peppercorn to your face. You may have to hold it in place while the glue sets. Don't glue it anywhere near your eyes—peppercorns and eyeballs don't mix.

beauty box

You will need:

1 cigar box (ask your friendly shopkeeper to save discarded ones for you, or search for old ones in thrift stores)

Good craft glue, such as Aleene's Tacky Glue

1 small mirror

Decoupage medium (available in craft stores)

Pictures of you and your friends, or magazine clippings

1 foam brush

Flatback rhinestones

[1] Get your cigar box and go to town. Begin by gluing on your mirror. We like ours on the inside of the hinged lid.

[2] Next, decoupage on your pictures or clippings. Just brush a little decoupage medium on the back of a picture, using the foam brush, and stick it on the cigar box. Brush more decoupage medium on top. Allow to dry, then add more coats of decoupage medium until you're satisfied with the shine. Be sure to allow the medium to dry between coats.

[3] Finish up by gluing on a healthy assortment of flatback rhinestones. Allow the glue to set before using.

Makes 1 beauty box

parties

Makeup is fun all by itself. Add a few friends, some streamers, and a bowl of potato chips, and you've got yourself a real wingding. Invite the whole posse over for a makeup-themed soirée. Here are a few of our favorites.

Cover Girl Photo Shoot Party

If you've got a digital camera and a few good friends, you've got everything you need for a photo shoot shindig. Stock the studio with lipsticks, eyeshadows, false eyelashes, and foundation. Go ahead and get the cheap stuff—it's only for one night. Paint yourselves up and snap away. The camera loves you, baby! Take five for fashionable little snacks like dim sum. When you're done, use your computer to turn your pictures into mock magazine covers. They'll make great party souvenirs. Your friends will have so much fun, you're sure to make the cover of *Best Hostess Monthly*.

Natural Beauty Spa Party

Did midterms take their toll? Is your skin dull and your nail polish chipped? You and your crew need to recharge your beauty batteries. Take a time out and host a Natural Beauty Spa Party. Give yourselves facials, manicures, and pedicures. When your polish is dry, make your own natural cosmetics, like Lip Fudge (page 103). Snack on indulgent homemade treats like warm cookies. Now, isn't that better? Naturally.

Makeup Olympics Party

If makeup were a competitive sport, you'd qualify for the gold. You can line lips and blend blush like nobody's business. It's time to test your skills with a Makeup Olympics Party. Stock up on crazy makeup and accessories like wigs, scarves, and feather boas. Then give your friends extreme makeovers. Transform your preppy princess friend into a goth creature of the night. Turn your tomboy friend into a disco diva glamour queen. When you're tired of making each other up, make up dinner. Let guests top their own mini pizzas. They'll give this party a ten.

the End